SELECTED LIVES

The Autobiography of a Soul

Written and illustrated by

Jasper Burns

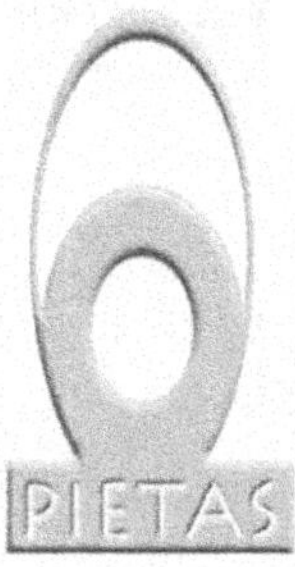

Copyright © 1986, 2006, 2013, 2017

Published by:

Pietas Publications
Waynesboro, Virginia, USA
web: www.jasperburns.com
email: pietas@jasperburns.com

THE LIVES

Imagine the Hindus, Buddhists, Pythagoreans, Orphics,
Theosophists, Essenes, Gnostics, Bantus, Jains,
and Platonists are right.

Imagine that an individual soul
inhabits many bodies,
lives many lives,
experiences many roles and places and times.

What would the autobiography of a soul be like?

Imagine you are a tiny blob of protoplasm,
adrift in the ocean, one billion years ago...

1. Cell division and death - 1 billion years ago

A blister of green
Squeezing through the stiff water
of a sun-washed sea;
Harvesting light.

*****

Pressure builds;
An explosion inside of me,
Splitting each particle and pore
As I shudder and dervish into two beings.

*****

Then a searing touch
from a living star,
and life leaves...

One of me.

2. Dancing death - 425 million years ago

My legs clutched the mud when I saw them.
Not a twitch as I watched my enemies
Dance all around me:
Their pearly shells pointing at the sky.

His great eye lingered as he passed overhead,
But his tentacles stayed in their sheaths:
For another purpose.

The suitors twirled in the moonlight,
Floating past the motionless giant
until she joined the dance:
The winner chosen.

Their tentacles merged.
One of his plunged a luminous globe,
deep into her pulsing body.

Their weightless shells
see-sawed in opposite directions,
then sped apart in silence.

And I had forgotten they were enemies.

3. A trilobite's new skin - 400 million years ago

My joints stiffen, my senses dim;
My mind lapses away.

*****

I awake to tightness, convulsions.
I draw my head under, arching my back
Splitting my skin.

*****

Crawling free, I swell and brighten.
I tingle with life once again.

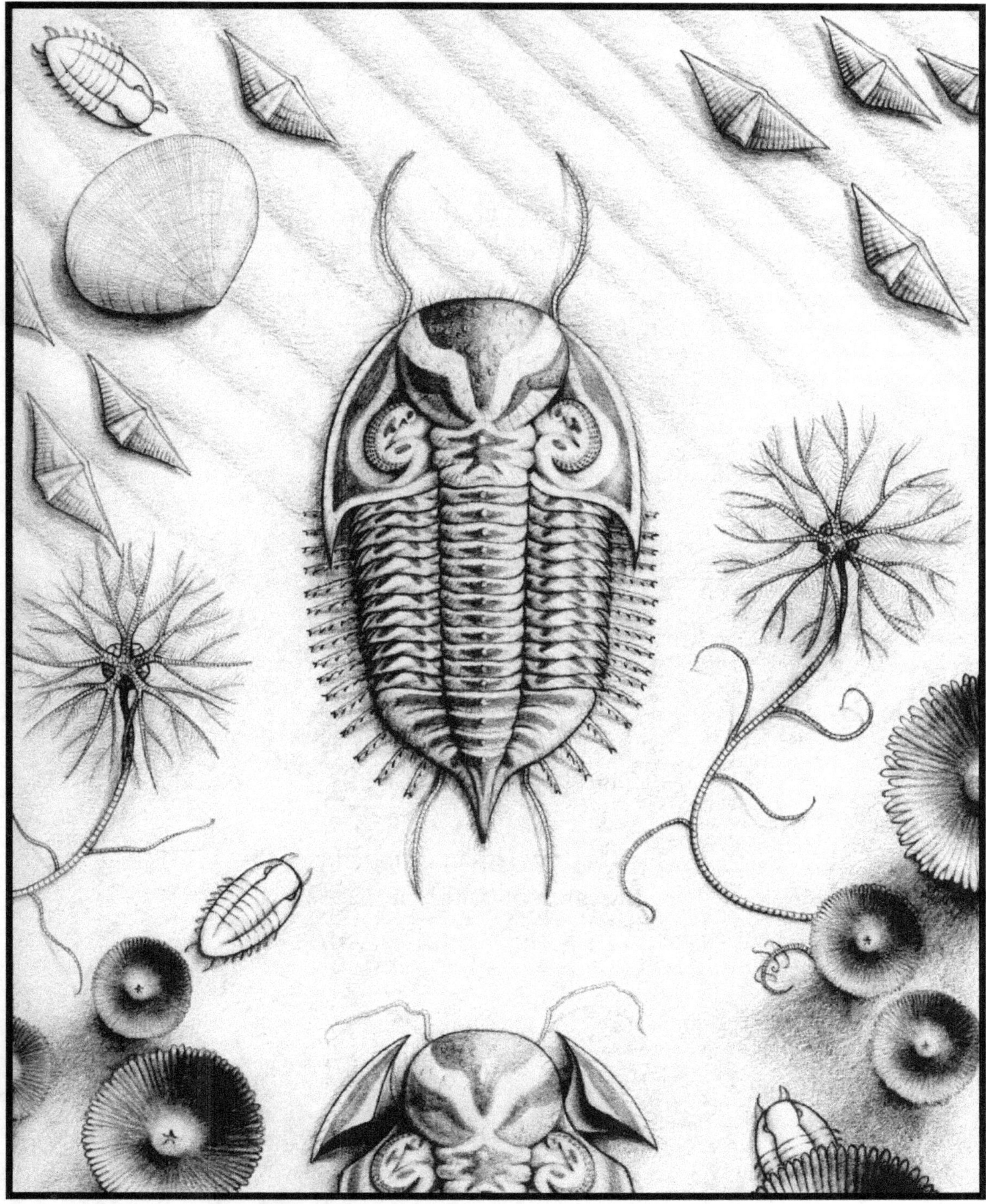

4. Arthropleura's fungal feast - 300 million years ago

I flow through the forest
on a river of legs.

Antennas twisting and groping,
The aroma beckoning.

*****

Days may be passing.
I know only the taste.

*****

At last I am sated,
My body filled,
Jaws straining to close.

I gather my legs and march:
In search of other meals.

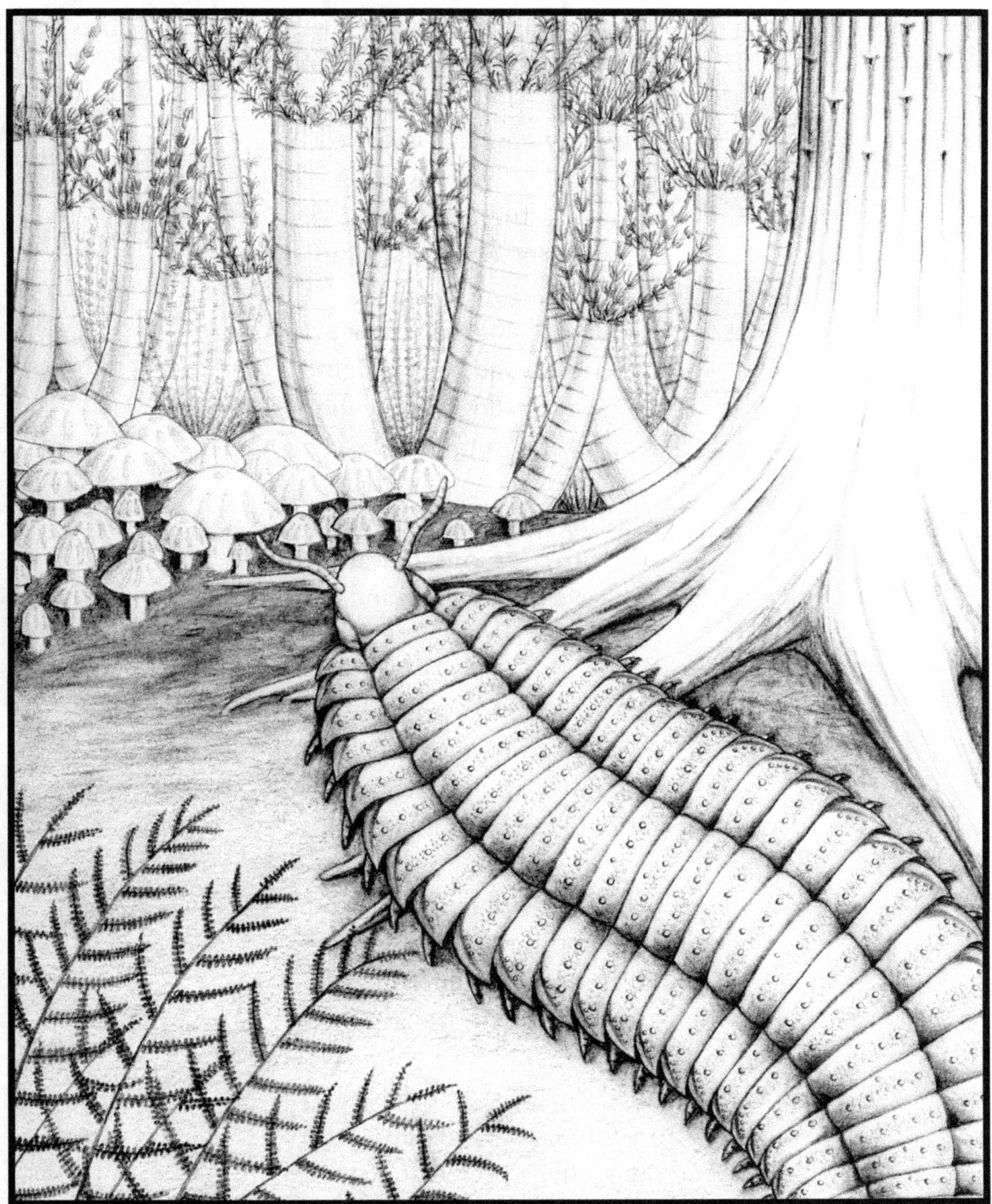

5. Day in the life of a coelacanth - 290 million years ago

When first my nostrils swallowed sky
from pools of viscous green,
The ripples stirred a dragonfly:
Two wisps of swirling steam.

I settled down beside a log,
And watched and felt for signs,
Of moving shadows in the fog,
Of shifting, surging tides.

A coasting turn, a sniff, a dash:
The current running near!
The murk gave way to glint and splash,
The misty sky grew clear.

I felt the bubbles curl around
My fins of rainbow hue.
I sank my teeth into the sound
Of twisting, writhing blue!

A belly taut with flesh and sand
Grew still in fading light,
And let my senses find the path
To waters safe at night.

I curled my tail with careful aim
into my jagged den.
And dragonfly appeared and claimed
His quiet perch again.

6. The Permian is for lovers - 275 million years ago

She stands by the bank of a lazy stream,
the light soft on her glittering skin.
I stare at her gold-rimmed eyes.
She blinks deeply in reply.
My mind folds gently around her.

A rival crashes between us.
I bare a hundred teeth at him,
but she winks her approval!

With jaws gaping, I charge!
We arch on sturdy legs,
Pouring hatred into each other's eyes.

He deflates with a long, low hiss
and skulks away.
I turn toward my gleaming prize,
Blowing bubbles from the corners of her mouth.

7. A close call - 240 million years ago

I awake in gentle stages,
nudged by breezes,
stirring my appetite.

I make for the shallows
to browse among the horsetails
and dry my back in the afternoon sun.

A chill dances across my shoulders:
There on the beach, waiting and watching:
Three demons!
Piercing my hide with their eyes!

8. Ginkgo harvested by a prosauropod – 210 million years ago

The rising sun burns the dew from my leaves.
I feel a surging effervescence;
My roots sucking earth through my veins.

My leaves track their Lord across the sky:
Swiveling and tilting with perfect care,
Gleaning vigor and growth from the rays,
Mixing the shimmering harvest with air -
Returning whispers.

With a sudden, violent twist,
The Sun jerks wildly above me.

My draining sap makes all clear:
Tis not the Sun at all, but I:
Plucked by a shadow!

9. Plundering plesiosaur - 200 million years ago

I feel fear before I see
The fluttering tails in front of me,

Or the speeding teeth behind.

The endless neck,
reeling like a waterspout,
bolting down our bright bodies,
leaving sparkles and puffs of blood.

10. Soaring pterosaur - 150 million years ago

The others preen and squabble,
Shaking the tree with their excitement.
Shrieks of society piercing the air.

With wide eyes and a racing heart,
I take an evening cruise.

Swoop and swerve, bank and fly,
Piling up air for its own sake,
Spiraling through heaven!

11. Apatosaurus surrounded by allosaurs - 145 million years ago

I watch my mother swallow a river,
And crane her neck into the sky.
Sniffing danger!

Her roar loosens pebbles from canyon walls.

The herd rumbles gradually into flight,
Losing me in the dust.

When it settles, I am alone
With three nightmares!

I hear the ripping sounds as they tear me open,
Talons scraping ribs,
My life seeping away…

12. Turtle landing - 100 million years ago

I plunge into the slurry,
Battered by waves of waves.

Sand clogging my eyes,
I snort onto the beach:
Dragging myself above the tides.

Flippers sweeping;
Hind legs reaching - deeply,
Scooping a pit in the cool earth.

With my whole being,
I force a single globe out of me,
And belch as dozens follow.

13. Toying with an inferior lifeform - 70 million years ago

A ball of fuzz squirms underfoot.
He runs for cover;
I stomp out his escape.

I study his face;
Squeeze a broken cry from his soft body.

Hissing loudly, I jump back:
Bitten by an insolent toy!

I kick him into the air
Catch him in my jaws.
Shake my head rapidly,
Back and forth;
My serrated teeth rip through tendon and flesh!

The taste of blood quenches my anger.
I watch him writhe in the dirt for a while,
His chest heaving,
Then race off;
No longer amused.

14. Revenge in reverse - 60 million years ago

My tongue tastes the evening,
Its sliver tips waving.
I slide from my den and swim through the shadows,
Slicing through reeds at the riverbend,
Threading the tangle-brush.

A musky scent: a possible meal!
But the smell grows too strong,
the shadow too deep.

I strike at him;
He backs away;
But then there are two!

They pounce and crush and tug and twist,
flinging me into a crumpled heap.

Finally, I see them leave,
with the eye that is able to see.

15. Odontopteryx hatching - 58 million years ago

Only an amber glow,
the soft thunder of my own pulse...

Then a song
Tugs at my heart,
Crystallizes my mind.

*****

Claustrophobia!
Straining,
Scraping against the unknown.

A sweet, chilly stream of air
flows through the jagged window.

I throw off the shards of oblivion.

16. Seven-foot cock of the walk - 50 million years ago

A dozen eyes are watching:
Time to make my play.

He stands his ground and crows from his toes.

We collide in mid-air,
Razor-claws groping for blood,
Hooked beaks lunging.

He rears on top!

With the last of my spirit,
I break free
and run for my life:

Dimly aware of a dozen eyes,
Turning down.

17. A primate's crunchy snack - 40 million years ago

Hand over hand,
Down the branch to the dangling fruit,
Both fists stuffing my mouth,
My lips smacking loudly.

I listen to the ocean of sound:
A million insects -
A million crunchy snacks.

I focus on a grating noise above me.
"Ch-ch-CHIT! Ch-ch-CHIT!"
Somewhere above me.

My senses swallow the darkness,
Leading me closer…

It stops - the final rasp ringing in my ears.
Pounce-grab-crunch!
My lips smacking loudly.

18. A freak storm - 30 million years ago

I stood up and snorted and shook myself clean,
Sniffing the cold morning air,
Then shuddered and blinked as I looked all around:
What was this white everywhere?

Rising in panic, the rest of the herd
Bellowed in fear and surprise,
Violently throwing the stuff from their backs,
Charging the flakes in the sky!

All of a sudden, the white ceased to fall;
The clouds were soon gone from the sky.
Never again did I see such a thing,
And never did I wonder why.

19. The grieving whale - 15 million years ago

A day away from the islands, I heard the cry
That our kind makes when we die.
This time, I recognized the voice:
This time it was my brother!

I sped for the waters of our birth,
My thoughts racing,
Pausing only when I breached
to renew my troubled breath.

Every year we would meet in the surf,
Leaping from the water,
Crushing the waves like thunder.

A flurry of fish draws my attention:
Shreds of flesh dancing to their nibbles;
His scarred and barnacled tail;
The tooth of a giant shark.

The sorrow stays in my heart.
I will never thunder in the waves again.

20. Strange beasts - 2 million years ago

Bizarre creatures -
Slicing through grass
like scorched giraffes.

Bodies shining like tar,
Stabbing the air with needle fingers,
Spitting streams of nonsense
through small white teeth.

Deranged cousins?
Or shadows alive!

21. King of the desert - 1 ½ million years ago

The drought makes them slower,
Less wary, less nimble -
Times are good!

I lock on a zebra, my paws drawing him closer,
Shoulder blades pumping as I glide forward,
Keeping time with my pounding heart.

Running, racing, bounding, leaping,
Digging my needles into his back,
Gouging the life out of him.

*****

After my nap, I stand up and stretch,
A wave arches through my spine
into a tongue-curling yawn.

I hear their murmurs, the scrawny beasts -
Stealing my honest meal!
I snag one with a claw,
Another with my fangs.

Bony meals for later, perhaps,
If the vultures leave any.

22. Gomphotheres caught by an Ice Age - 1 million years ago

The snows are early - nothing to eat.

We march to the winter valley,
Our trunks puffing fog.

A blizzard drives the youngest to her knees.
We coax and caress her.
But she blinks at the snowflakes and dies.

At last the final ridge,
The valley before us...

I rear up and pummel the sky;
Our green meals,
Stolen by the wind!

23. Musing by the campfire - 200,000 years ago

The blaze begins to speak:
The words unknown, but tender,
Like shelling nuts in the evening,
Or laughing by a waterfall.

The flames work along a twig
like a herd of purple reindeer,
Antlers jerking and swaying.

I watch myself explore the flames,
Frolicking in the piles of ash,
Entering caves of liquid light.

I remember a thousand fires,
And faces,
Wild sparkles in their eyes.

24. Neanderthal wedding - 75,000 years ago

My father bargains with Snow Wolf:
The two of them toe to toe -
Their massive arms folded across their chests.
They are talking about me.

I hear my father say, "Killer of Cave Bear."
I had forgotten - I have become a man!

I fold my arms across my chest.

Snow Wolf approaches me.
"We have decided. You will marry my daughter."

We sit before the mammoth skull,
Surrounded by tusks and autumn flowers.
The others dance and sing
as I study her eyes, her skin,
Glowing like flint in the sun.

I can feel our spirits mingling.

25. Neanderthal dream – 50,000 years ago

I stir to the smell of salt air
and the hissing, thundering, fizzing surf.

I tell the rhino how much I love the sea.
I should be surprised when he agrees,
But I'm not.

We watch the gulls soar and glide.
To my surprise, rhino hides diaphanous wings,
within his heavy fur.

I lose him in a cloud and float free,
Then begin to fall – too fast!

I slam my head against the wall of the cave
as I awake gasping.

26. Staying behind – Europe, 35,000 years ago

My mother sobs as she rolls up the tent skins:

"Grandma is staying behind.
She says she is ready to join the ancestors."

"Yes, child. It is true; I can go no farther.
The time has come for me to see the next world,
Where it is warm and happy and food abounds."

She closes her eyes and smiles,
As if glimpsing that place.

I pull the skin close against the stinging cold.

"Take me with you, Grandmother!
Take me to the world of warmth and laughter!"

That afternoon we move on,
Struggling through the snow.

And every time I turn to see,
She smiles and sheds a tear - for me.

27. The first fishhook – Europe, 30,000 years ago

I'm making needles;
Carving them from reindeer bone.

They pile up like fish skeletons at a feast.

My mind wanders.
I have a vision:

A curved needle at the end of a line…

28. Shaman's song – Europe, 20,000 years ago

After the hunt, I collapse by the fire:
in no mood for ceremony.
But Shaman hands me the drum.
The Mother must be thanked!

"Deep in the caves, dark of your womb,
We painted the seeds of his birth.
Return now this beast to our hunting ground.
Restore him to roam o'er the Earth."

As they skin the animal,
Lay fresh meat on the coals,
Shaman tears off his clothes,
Dancing naked in the fire.
His voice ringing in the starry sky:

"Bless the sinews of our prey,
Give his strength to us today,
Make our hearts and bodies thine,
Mother! Make our food divine!"

29. Arms race on the Nile – Egypt, 10,000 B.C.

They ignore our warnings, our sacred claims.
Small men with flimsy weapons,
Against our stout spears and spirits!

Their leader raises his stick like a magic wand.
It spits a pointed shaft into our leader's chest.
And another as he spins to the ground.
Each time a twang, a low wicked whistle,
And "chutf" as it punctures skin.

We hurl our spears,
Dropping two of the demons,
But watch helpless as they raise their wands,
Again and again,
And we have nothing to return.

They burn our huts, splinter our gods,
Take our women.

I want to fight again, but remember:
The twang, the low wicked whistle,
The "chutf" as it punctures skin.

30. Giant armadillo surrounded in Texas - 9000 B.C.

A boulder-bear!

He lunges at us, snorting,
Swinging his great pine cone of a tail.
Then pulls into his shell,
Thinking he can outwait us.

We rush to his side,
Using our spears to flip him over,
Dodging his hammer-claws,
Gouging out his racing heart!

Cheerfully, we cut up the meat.

Nothing tastes better than boulder-bear.
And nothing is more fun to hunt!

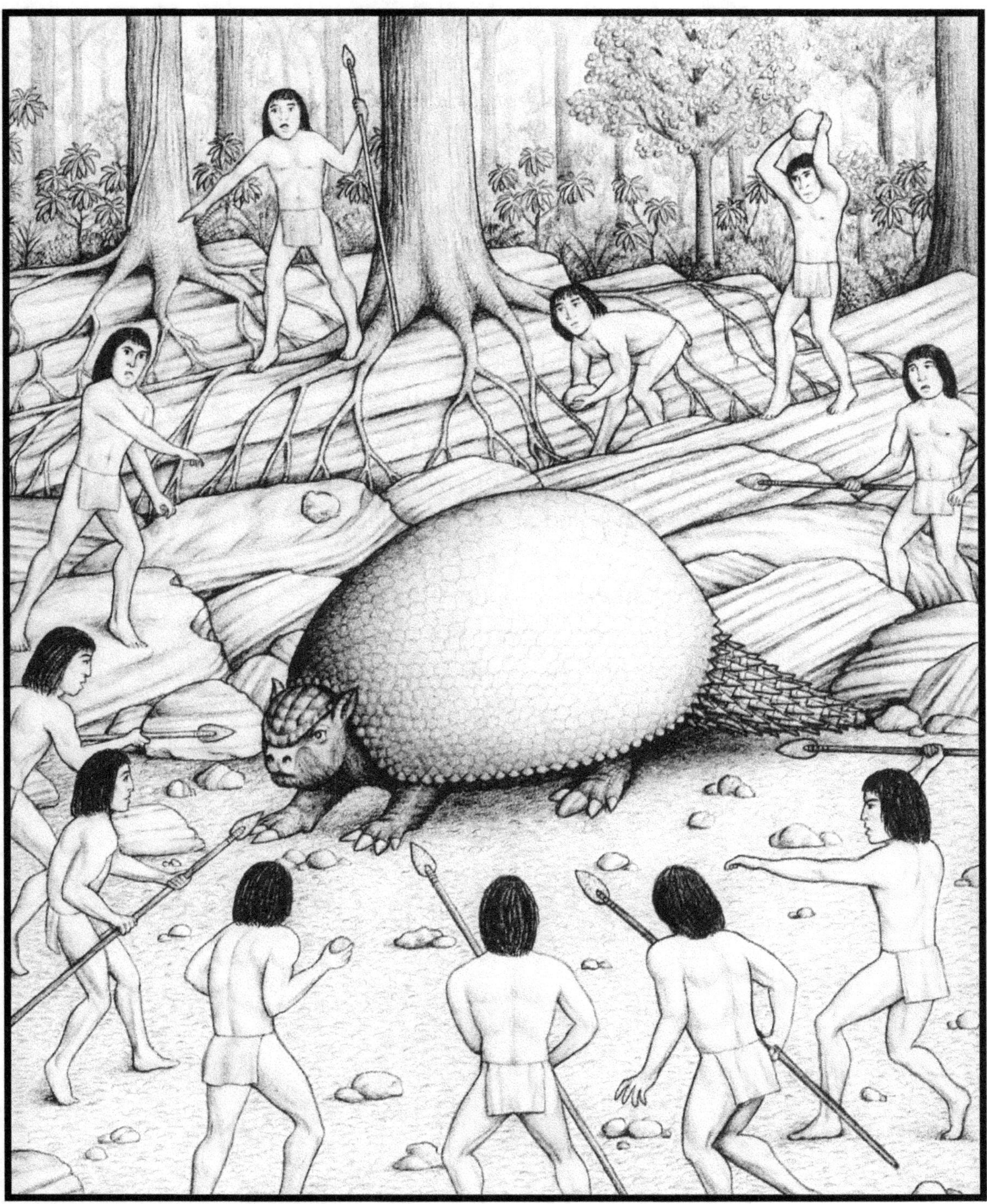

31. The first walls of Jericho - 7500 B. C.

We remembered the savages.
They came from the mountains;
They took everything they could carry.

So when our leader told us to build a wall;
We built a wall.

When it was done, we feasted;
We marvelled at what we had done.

I stood on top of the edifice
and spied a swarm of campfires
at the foot of the mountains.

Next morning, five hundred wildmen
Looked up at our wall in wonder.

32. Potter's lesson – Hacilar, Turkey, 5500 B.C.

Slowly molded from the finest clay –
What a price this bowl will bring!

I worry and watch as it shrinks and dries,
singeing my brow as I coax the fire.

*****

Never since have I let cunning
Thoughts of gain debase my art;
Never since have I left running
with an armful of my heart!

33. The Mountain Spirit's face – eastern North America, 4500 B.C.

I find it on top of the mountain,
Sparkling with crystals,
Shining like stars,
Urging me to commune with its spirit.

My eyes vibrate across the grooved surface,
The grinning eyes and pointed chin.

For a moment, I can feel the mountain breathe!

I heap a few stones around it - a holy place:
The shrine of the mountain spirit's face.

34. Along the Yellow River – China, 4000 B.C.

A calm bright day at last!
I send the children to fill the water jugs.

I am in front, breaking earth, eating dust,
Cheering as my muscles warm.

Behind, my wife sprinkling seeds:
Golden millet from practiced hands.

Then my son dribbling water.
And the young ones,
Tamping with tiny feet,
Their steps too light to trap the seeds.

Too soon, the seed is sown:
Planted in the sacred ground,
Sprinkled with the river,
The sweat of our hands and toes,

And prayers to coax each grain awake,
To flourish for our family's sake.

35. Following the king - Uruk, 3100 B. C.

It was hard enough losing a father;
Now my mother was joining him.

To drink the cup of poison,
to follow in my father's wake,
meant eternal life in honey-sweet Dilmun:
Abode of the blessed.

To let the cup pass
meant misery on Earth,
and, almost certainly:
Passage to dreaded Kur,
bleak city of the dead.

My mother didn't hesitate:
She drank deeply, quivering with pride.
But I could not follow;

Better the hell one knows
than the Paradise one imagines.

36. Flight from Malta - 3000 B.C.

"Build a new goat trough.
Plaster the side wall.
My husband is content to waste his time.
No wonder I suffer!
My sister laughs at my poverty.
My children wonder what they will eat."

I take ship and sail away from her nagging,
Trying to forget her parting words:

"You will be cursed by the misery of your children;
Their faces will haunt you forever!"

I see the wonders of Egypt, of Italy and Crete.
But each day I remember:
The misery of my children.
Fatherless faces,
Haunting me forever.

37. The God-King – Egypt, 2600 B.C.

I watch him glide into the temple,
His movements graceful and strange,
As if the Nile itself courses through his veins.
It is Khufu, the living god!

I sink to my knees and watch,
Holding my breath until I can no longer,
Then breathing quick silent gasps,
Waves of excitement washing through me.

I sink further as he kneels before his father's statue,
Then spreads himself flat on the floor,
His nose and lips and kneecaps
Pressing against the cold alabaster.
Again, I hold my breath.

He rises and departs,
Leaving the air fragrant, vibrating.

A pool of tears overfills each eye,
My fingertips tremble.
I spread myself flat on the floor.

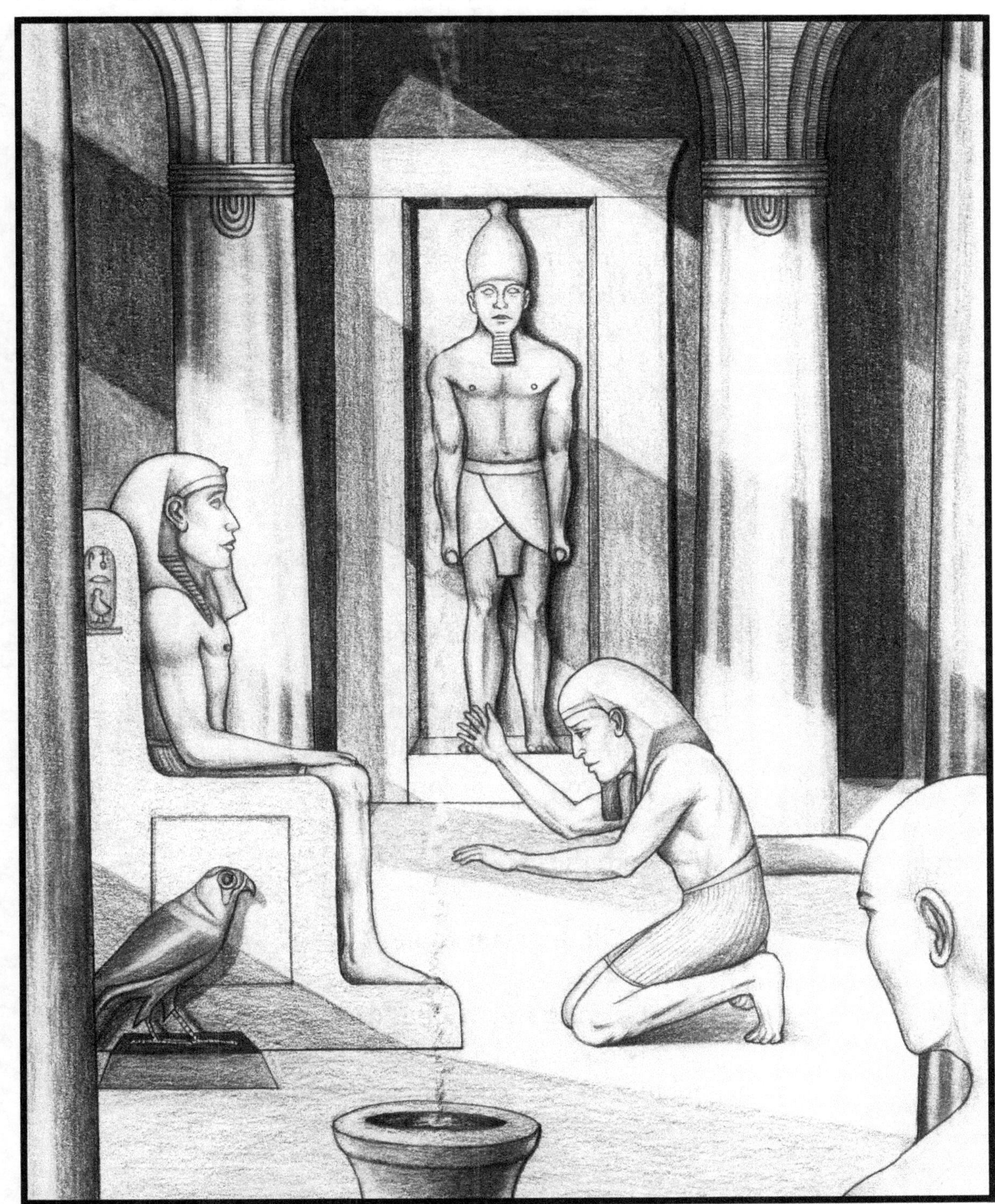

38. Drought – northeast Africa, 2200 B.C.

The desert rising, swallows my pastures.
Skimming the fat from my beasts.
I grind my teeth and watch the cloudless sky.

I will remain strong!

The calves weaken, stiff-legged;
Their mother's udders - dry.
I slaughter the newborn,
Washing their flesh down with tears.

But I will remain strong.

The water holes are empty,
The trails lined with corpses.
My cows are dropping,
I lift them up - they sink again,
Into the gathering sand.

Still, I remain strong.

My herd is gone; the world is deserted -
Only bones and a lonely man,
Dragging his feet sideways through the dunes.

39. Melanesian homecoming, 2000 B.C.

Our hearts swell like sails
as we enter virgin seas:
Looking for a new home.

No island swells or birds for days.
Our food and water dwindle –
Children fret as I spy the dogs.

At last, the night waves flashing,
Speak of shores unseen,
Confirmed by ripples and floating weeds.

At last we see:
Emerald cliffs;
White featherfalls of sweet water;
Coconut palms waving a welcome ashore.

We splash into our new world;
the shaded sand cool beneath my feet.

40. Minoan melancholy - 1500 B.C.

Chilled by a drizzle in my soul, I consider my life.

My palace, my dream rendered in stone:
Nudged by quakes, its colors fading like the dream.

My strength, now ebbing, unsure of its effect,
As brittle as my wrinkled fist.

My optimism, tempered by reason;
The mine too deep for surprises.

My mind, the victim of its own cleverness,
Lost in a labyrinth of its own designs.

Some say I am divine, a god on earth.
Once I might have believed,
When clouds seemed to part for my passing.

But would a god's mind be so tortured
Or heart be so cold as mine?

41. On an Indian plain - 1000 B. C.

At first I am a whirlwind,
But my passion wanes.
Now barely able to grip the sword,
My wrist smarting with each blow.

The next morning, we hold back,
Our insides writhing like snakes.

The prince drives to the fore,
His words finding our hearts:

"We are soldiers! To our duty!
He who dies in battle, fighting bravely,
Conquers Death forever!"

Our spirits rise like a river!
Suddenly this hideous business
Seems like the play of Nature herself:

A squall of humanity, spending itself on the plain.
And we are God's minions,
Like drops of rain,
Running to a peaceful sea.

42. Olmec delinquent - 800 B.C.

Torn from the magic jungle,
Thrown into the land of stones,
To learn rituals!

What do I care for rituals?
Endless ceremonies in the broiling sun,
ordered about by bloated priests.

The night of my escape, I leave my mark!
Picturing their horrified frowns,
Their huffs and their puffs.

I swear I will never be old or boring like them!

43. Meeting Pythagoras – Italy, 530 B.C.

He scans the crowd,
reading each face like a scroll.
Then I realize he is staring at me!
I have come to see the great Pythagoras;
Not be seen *by* him!

"People come from all parts of the world.
They ask: 'Who am I? Where am I going?'
'What is the purpose of life?'

"I tell them:
'You are a divine spark from the fire of God.'
'You have given life to countless bodies,
forgetting your true nature.'
'The purpose of life is to know yourself;
To find your way home.'"

I flush with shame;
I have spent my life in pursuit of moments,
as if I would never die,
until death, like a shadow, creeps toward me.

I ask: "How may we know
That we have lived before,
And may live again?"

"By promises unfulfilled,
Justices undone, powers unearned,
And strangers known as friends.
How else do you explain
Wise children and old fools?"

I grieved for a life wasted.
But at least now I knew - that I was an old fool.

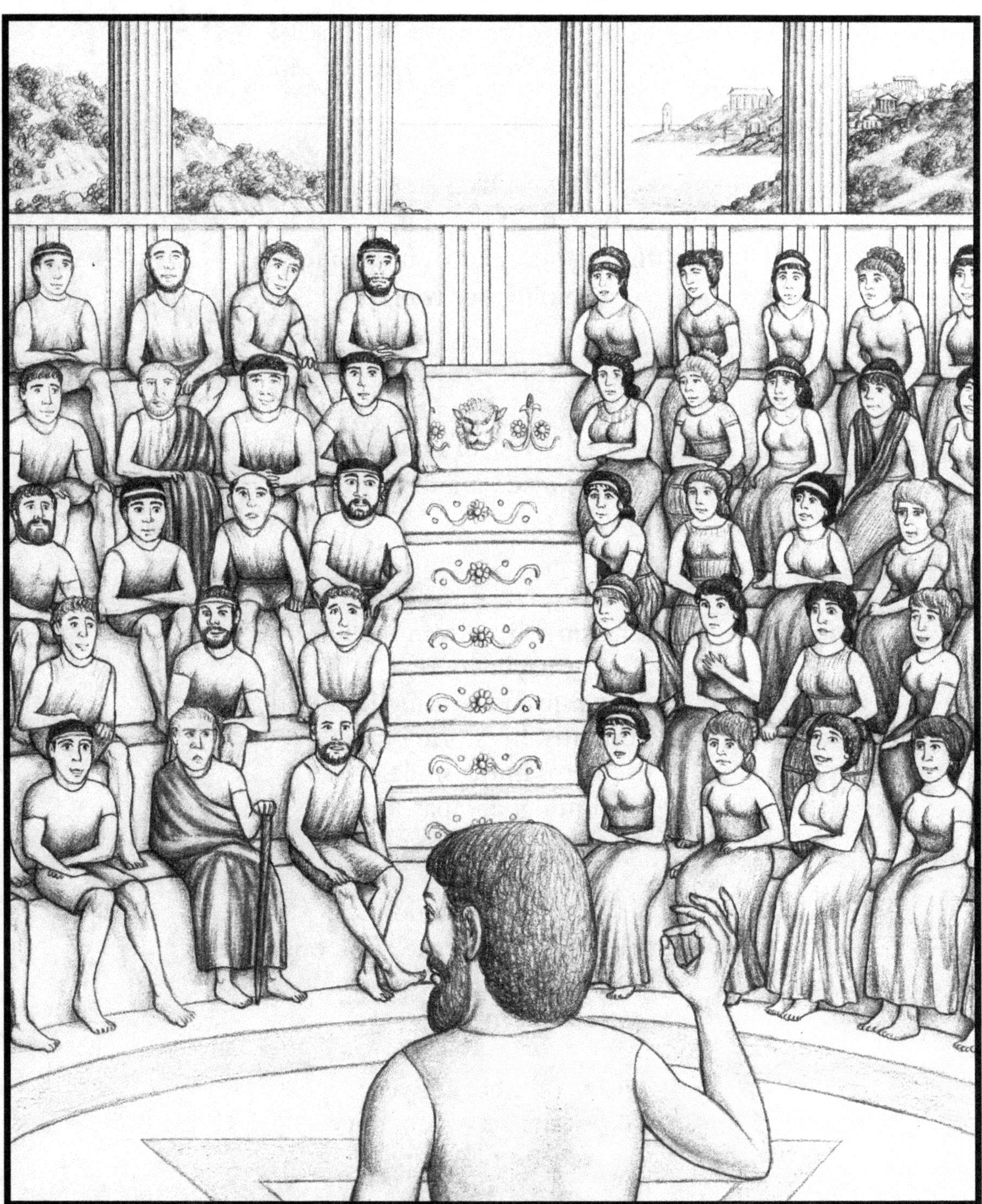

44. Jesus in the temple - Jerusalem, A.D. 29

Who is this maniac?
Berserk in the temple,
Overturning our tables, our businesses,
Spilling our coin?

"It is written,
'My house shall be called
The House of Prayer.'
But you have made it a den of thieves!"

*****

I gather my share from the floor
(maybe more)
And follow him to a waiting multitude.
Instantly, his stormy brow
leaps into a smile.
Welcoming, compassionate:
Like a mother waking babies.

I ask his companions:
"How can he find peace in the blink of an eye?
My hands still tremble,
My face burns with rage."

One of them answers:
"Our master serves not anger;
Anger serves him!"

45. Mayan home cooking - A.D. 400

Weeks of temple food give me a jittery belly,
Twisting moods and tortured nights:

Peppers stuffed with ground puppy,
Boa brains dipped in honey:
Cooked to cajole the spirits,
Seasoned with desire.

Food made for the gods!

*****

I slip away to my mother's home,
Begging a meal:

Corn cakes burping steam on the hot stone.
Beans, tomatoes, squash simmering.
Simple fare from honest hands,
Nourishing body, heart, and soul.

Food fit for the gods!

46. Mother of the world – India, A.D. 800

Chosen by the priests
to be Lakshmi in the festival.

I remember my childish crimes
And feel unworthy.

When the day arrives,
They whisper in my ear:

"Remember, you are Mother of the whole world."

I sit as still as I can,
Balancing the heavy crown,
Receiving the worshipers' gifts and prayers.

I see their longing, their devotion, their tears.

Somewhere deep inside,
I feel love flowing.

The priests were right;
I am their mother after all!

47. A woman's path – Egypt, 1200

It is better to be a man, isn't it Mother?
They do not work so hard as women.

"But work keeps the mind pure and the body strong."

"Is it not better to be master than slave?"

"Not if the master sinks into arrogance, or laziness.
It is better to serve than to swell with pride."

"But doesn't pride build character?"

"Not if it restrains compassion, for fear of appearing weak.
Or prevents candor, for fear of losing face.
Or keeps one from laying one's heart at God's feet."

"So it is better to be a woman?"

"Either path is strewn with thorns and flowers,
And neither is well-travelled,
Until it reaches God's door.
Then both man and woman leave the path behind."

48. Boomerang – Australia, 1400

"A man must understand the ways of the boomerang."

I watch my uncle fling it just above the earth.
It bursts skyward, like a lorikeet surprised,
Whirling in a wide circle before us,
Landing like a feather at our feet.

I try again and again:
It stumbles and dies, slaps into a tree,
Bounces high and lands on my head.

"I cannot do it, Uncle."

"That is correct.
Now,
Let the boomerang do it!"

I understand. I relax. I loosen.
I feel my body turn.
It lets go of me.

My fingertips follow its flight.
Soaring like a lorikeet,
Spinning, circling,
Landing like a feather at our feet.

49. Elizabethan justice – London, 1600

A priest is in my cell,
His eyes pacing the floor.
I killed a man. I will go to Hell.
So he believes. So I believe.

*****

The executioner stares at me,
His eyes sparkling through his hood.

"So you will send me to Hades?"

"Is that where you want to go?"

"What choice do I have? I have sinned."

"Can you remember innocence?"

I can. I do. For a moment, I am pure again.

"That is your soul, my friend.
Your soul knows nothing of your crime.
Leave your body to its wretched fate,
But follow your soul to Heaven!"

50. Freedom – Virginia, 1800

I watch the old master, walking with Joe.

Master waits for whims to plan his day;
Joe always breaks a sweat before the sun rises.

Master is like the weather:
Storming or listless or breezy or dry;
Joe is too busy to notice moods.

Master is proud of his name,
Demanding respect from all he meets;
Joe gets no respect at all, and needs none -
To respect himself, and everyone.

Master fears ruin,
Nervously tracing the books -
Terrified - of living like Joe,
While Joe lives without fear.

And I wonder:
When will the master be free?

51. A ray of light – Virginia, 1900

What solace is there
for a man whose soul mate is gone?

The dry wind moans,
The cedars shudder,
My spirit puckers and aches.
I ask God for one more glimpse.

There comes a vision:
Her eyes!
Brimming with love and compassion.
And then...
Her eyes become Christ's!

As soft as awaking, I understand:

The spirits I love and I worship,
Always were, will be, are truly -
One!

52. Depression – New York, 1945

How long must a man live in this world
Before a rose smells of the corpses caught on its thorns?

And a child's eyes seem to bear the seeds of bondage,
Of hatreds glimmering, of miseries unsuspected?
Till a baby's grin makes a man cringe in pity?

Before a young woman's face withers in his mind:
The lines and cares of sorrows to come
Tracing deeper, wearing away her innocent smile?

And his fellow men, grinding each other's souls away,
Sprouting horns and tails as they gird themselves
For business and war?

Till God seems a dream of the feeble-minded,
The weak and the frightened?

How long must a man live before he tires of it all,
As if he's lived a billion years?

53. Epiphany – Virginia, 1980

I don't believe in saints, or gods
Or anything, I like to think.

But I trust my senses, and my thoughts.

So what can I do when I am swept away
By a river of joy surging through me?

When I see lights more beautiful than stars,
Hear sounds too sweet for this world,
Smell fragrances worn by a goddess?

What can I do when my love overflows
For all times, all places, all beings?

When my life is emptied of sorrow and pain,
Confusion and shame,
And becomes a blissful journey
Home?

What can I do, but believe?

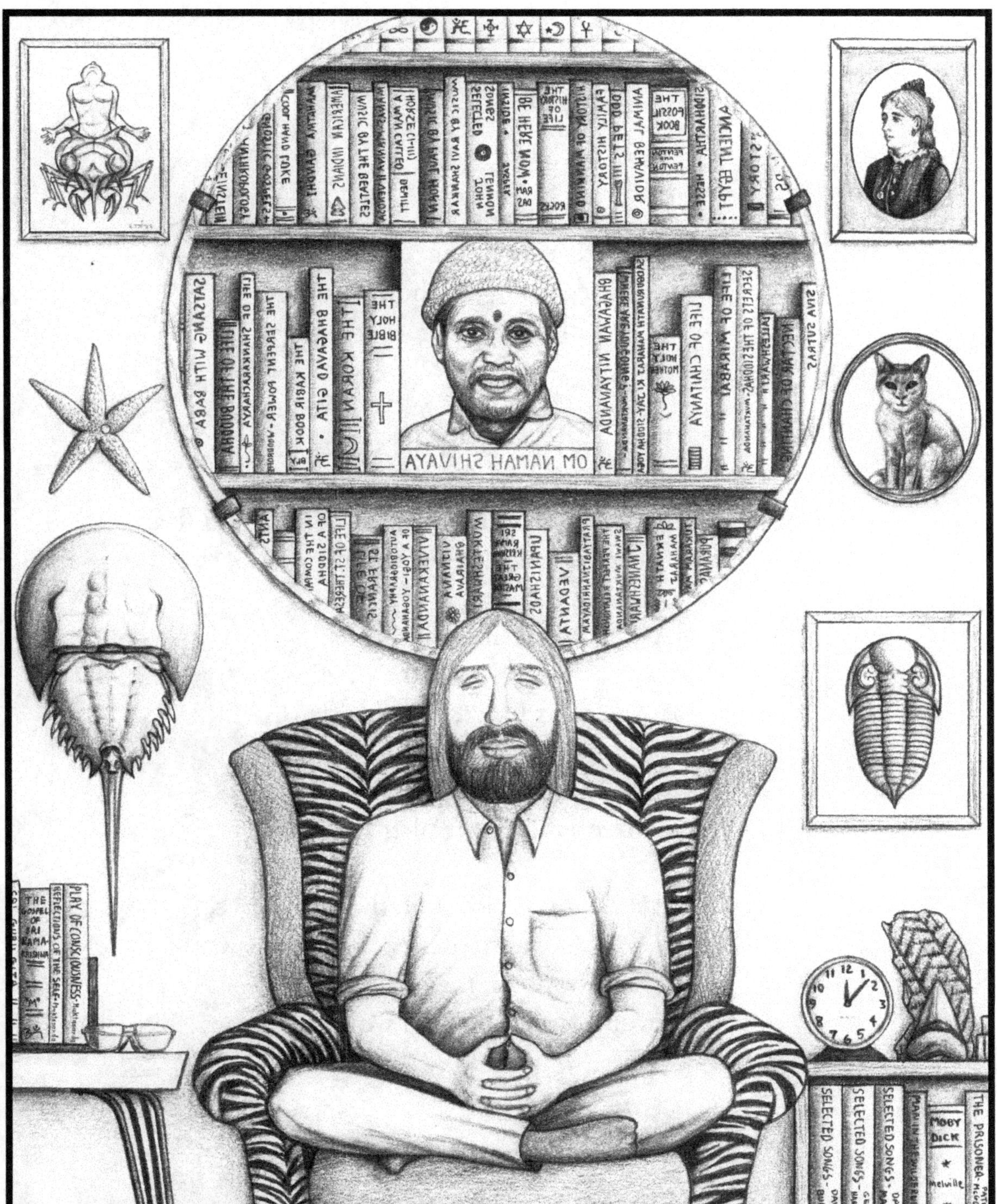

54. HOME

I am
Every where, every time, every thing:
Without beginning, without ending,
Unchanging
Bliss.

I am the Actor and the stage.
I assume all roles and all bodies.
As father, mother, and child, king and slave, fish and flea,
It is I that move and think and breathe.

As the bird I sing and flutter,
As the hunter I raise the bow,
As the shaft I pierce the heart.

As the bound soul I forget my nature,
As the free soul I remember it again.

My nature is unlimited joy, unfathomable love,
Pure awareness:
The source of all, the goal of all.
Beyond forms, beyond words,
Am I.

More by Jasper Burns

INSIDE

———

FOSSIL DREAMS

———

WISDOM ILLUSTRATED

———

SEEING GOD: CLOSE ENCOUNTERS OF THE DIVINE KIND

———

AUTO-BOOKS-OGRAPHY

———

ANIMAL OBITUARIES

———

THE NECESSARY NERD

———

THE 'ARCHAIC SMILE' AND GREEK COINS

———

COMMODUS AND THE FIVE GOOD EMPERORS

———

Many other titles on a variety of subjects